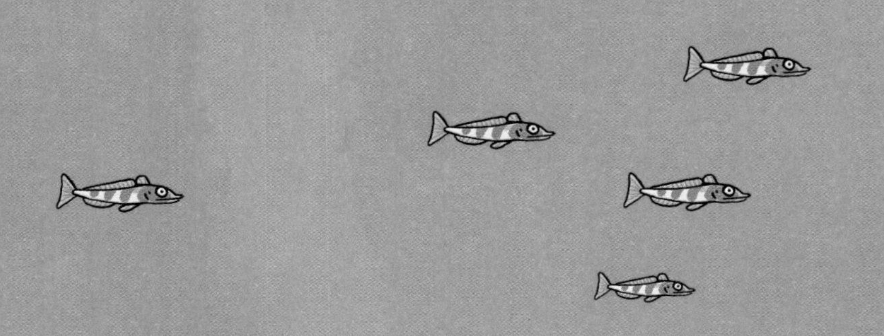

USBORNE

24 Hours in Antarctica

Andy Prentice

Illustrated by Laurent Kling

Designed by Jamie Ball

Consultants:

Dr. Joanne Johnson

Dr. Joanne Johnson is a geologist at British Antarctic Survey.

Professor David Vaughan

Professor David Vaughan is a glaciologist, and former Director of Science at British Antarctic Survey.

Usborne Quicklinks

For links to websites with videos and activities where you can find out more about what it's like to live and work in Antarctica, go to usborne.com/Quicklinks and type in the title of this book.

Here are some of the things you can do at the websites we recommend:

- Find out what life is like living at a research station.
- Watch the southern lights, or *aurora australis*, in Antarctica's night sky.
- Watch mother emperor penguins find their chicks.
- See what a blizzard can be like for some scientists in Antarctica.
- Find out what to wear to work in Antarctica.

Please follow the online safety guidelines at Usborne Quicklinks. Children should be supervised online. Usborne Publishing is not responsible for the content of external websites.

CONTENTS

Go swimming with penguins on page 14.

Did you know that Antarctica used to be covered in rainforest? Find out more on page 21.

Who were the first people to visit the South Pole? Find out on page 51.

7:15 a.m. November 29th
Antarctica
Rothera Station
1°C (33°F)

All is calm. All is quiet.
Here, at the extreme south of the world,
the Sun has been shining all night.
Rothera Station is waking up.

Comms (communications) tower
Science labs
Vehicle store
Generator
Carpentry workshop

Rothera is British Antarctic Survey's main research station. In the summer just over one hundred people live and work here. Just twenty-two remain for the winter.

BEEEEP
BEEEEEP
BEEEEEP
BEEEEEP
BEEEEEP
BEEEEEP
7:15 A.M.

7:16 A.M.
GOOD MORNING. I'm Viv!

I wear this eye mask to sleep. It's summer here in Antarctica and the Sun doesn't set.
You have to pack light, so only a few of your most important possessions can be brought to Antarctica.
7:19 A.M.

So BRIGHT! Ach!
Sunlight reflected off snow is dazzling.

I only flew in last week. I can't get over this view!

I bet you're wondering what I'm doing here? Well, it's not for the reasons that you might expect...
I'm not an explorer like these intrepid pioneers.
And I'm not a scientist like the people below, who are here to do experiments.

Roald Amundsen
Led the first team to reach the South Pole in 1911.

Robert Falcon Scott
His team reached the South Pole second, five weeks after Amundsen. He died in Antarctica.

Ann Bancroft
The first woman to walk across the ice to the North and South poles.

Geologist – taking samples from a rock carried miles by the ice.

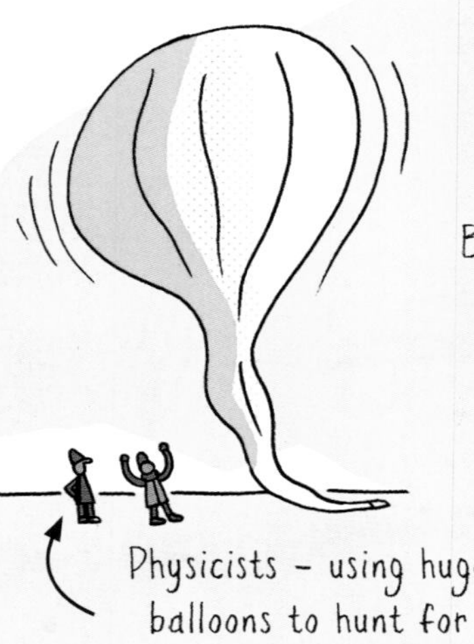

Physicists – using huge balloons to hunt for particles from space.

Biologist – observing penguins nesting.

Climate scientist – drilling for ancient ice.

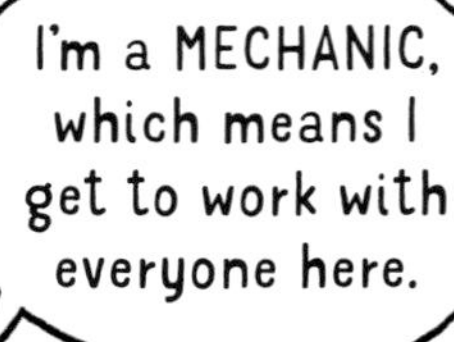

I'm a MECHANIC, which means I get to work with everyone here.

7:45 a.m.
Canteen
Surviving out here takes teamwork. EVERYONE has a vital job to do.
Chef
Sausages are ready!
Antarctica is VAST. The best way to get around is to fly.
Pilot
Boatman
Most food is delivered to Rothera by a boat that only comes once a year. It's a big order!
In the summer, fresh ingredients can arrive by plane every few weeks.
Computer specialist
Carpenter
Field guide – a survival expert who keeps everyone safe out on the ice.
Mobile phones don't work here, so people use walkie-talkies instead.
DISASTER! Breakfast's ruined...
Oh NO! The toaster's broken.
Doctor – treats many emergencies as there's no hospital for miles.
Geologist
What's that smell?
Station leader
Lab assistant

We're THOUSANDS of miles away from the nearest shop. So we have to make do with what we've got.
Are you using that pen?
THIS should do the trick.
CLICK
There we go! Good as new.
Thanks Viv! That's GENIUS.
POP
A classic British breakfast
Tea
Roast tomatoes
Sausages
Eggs
Mushrooms
Bacon
Baked beans
Coffee
EAT BIG! We need all our STRENGTH for the football match against the Spanish research ship later!

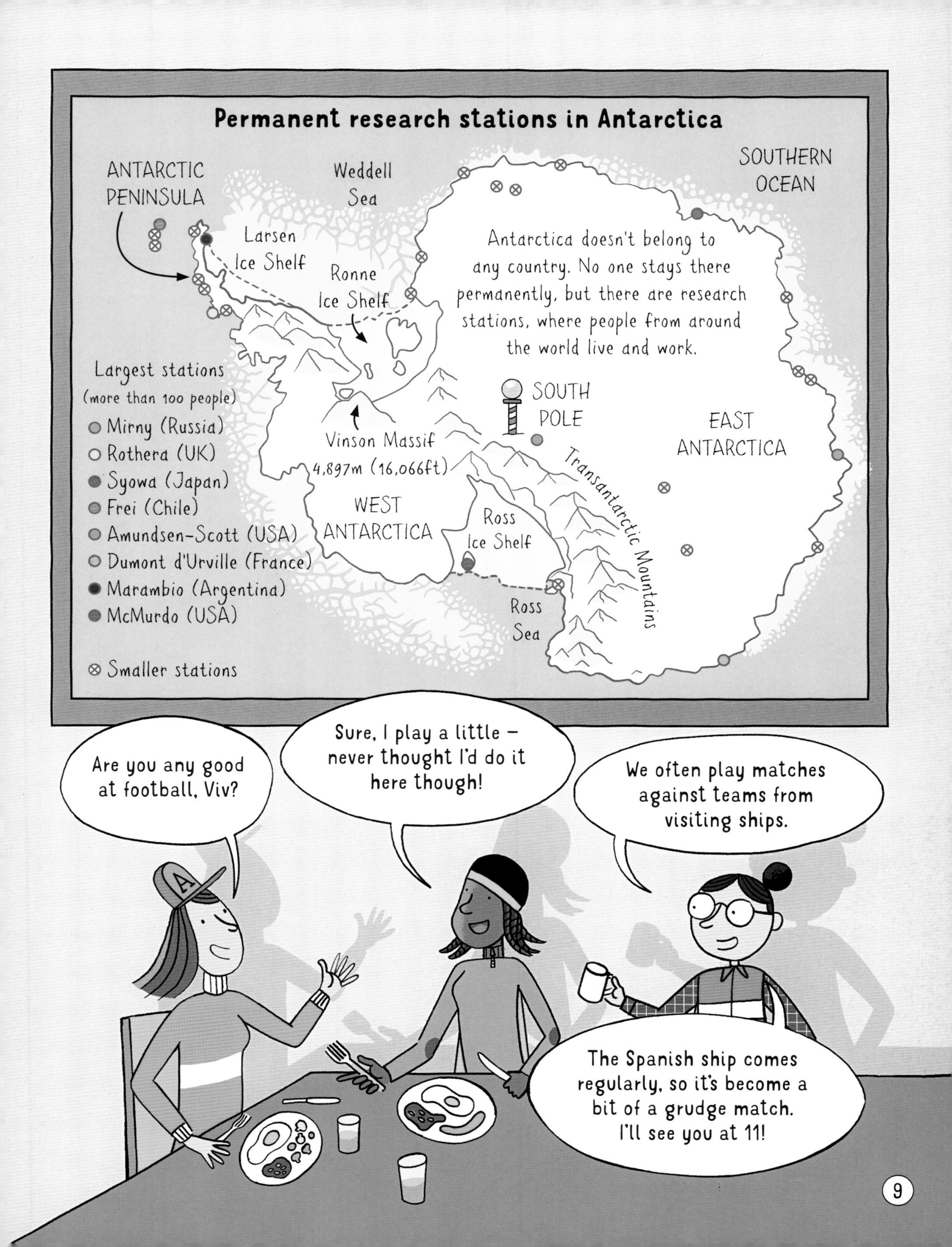
Permanent research stations in Antarctica
ANTARCTIC PENINSULA
Weddell Sea
SOUTHERN OCEAN
Larsen Ice Shelf
Ronne Ice Shelf
Antarctica doesn't belong to any country. No one stays there permanently, but there are research stations, where people from around the world live and work.
Largest stations (more than 100 people)
Mirny (Russia)
Rothera (UK)
Syowa (Japan)
Frei (Chile)
Amundsen-Scott (USA)
Dumont d'Urville (France)
Marambio (Argentina)
McMurdo (USA)
Smaller stations
SOUTH POLE
Vinson Massif 4,897m (16,066ft)
EAST ANTARCTICA
WEST ANTARCTICA
Transantarctic Mountains
Ross Ice Shelf
Ross Sea
Are you any good at football, Viv?
Sure, I play a little – never thought I'd do it here though!
We often play matches against teams from visiting ships.
The Spanish ship comes regularly, so it's become a bit of a grudge match. I'll see you at 11!

8:30 a.m.
Bonner Marine Research Lab
1° Celsius (33°F)

Morning! I heard you needed my help.
Thank goodness you've come Viv!
Our dive radio is broken.
Dive supervisor
Divers getting ready to study the seafloor

Do you think it will take long to fix? Forecast says there are heavy storms coming, so we need to make the most of this fine, "dingle" weather.
Oh no! Is that a SEAL?
False alarm! It's just a shadow.
No problem, looks like an easy fix.
Seal watch looks out for orcas and leopard seals.

Hang on. Why wouldn't you want to dive with seals?
They can be dangerous, especially leopard seals.
They've even ATTACKED small boats!

BRRR! It's cold. Can't imagine jumping into that water.
TWIST
You think this is COLD? In the winter we have to cut holes in the sea ice with chainsaws so we can dive.
Although the air isn't freezing, the wind makes it chilly.
Divers use special dry suits to stay warm in the frosty water.

Diving in winter
Sea temperature 1.8°C (35°F)
We always cut two holes in case a seal takes one over and traps us underwater.

Can't believe you go diving here in WINTER.
What else do you do? PICNICS?
HONK
HONK
Ha! NO – but maybe you'll see.
Are you just here for the summer, Viv? Or are you doing a whole year?
Oh, I'm here for the full year! What's winter like?
Antarctic Seasons
There are only two seasons in Antarctica. Winter runs from March until October. It is summer for the rest of the year.
Well... it's long... and it's dark...
At the end of May, the Sun sets...
At Rothera, the flag is lowered and won't be raised for two months until the Sun rises again.

And it's very, VERY cold...
...but it's also amazing!
Temperatures get so low that if you throw a cup of boiling water in the air, it instantly freezes.
The Southern Lights glow like vast fireworks in the sky.
In June, we throw a massive party to celebrate Midwinter Eve. It's a proper FEAST.
A
But what sticks with you is the incredible QUIET. So few of you, in this vast, frozen world.
Well, no more quiet for you! I've fixed your radio!

Underwater wildlife

Krill

In summer, tiny creatures called krill form big swarms. Krill are really important because they are eaten by almost everything – fish, seals, whales and penguins.

Crabeater seals

Are the most common type of seal in the world. Despite their name, they mostly eat krill, not crabs.

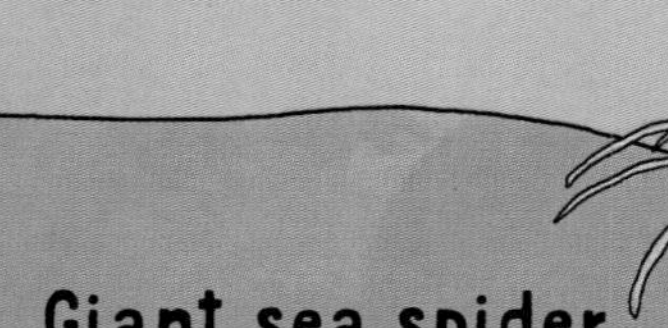

Icefish

These fish produce antifreeze in their blood.

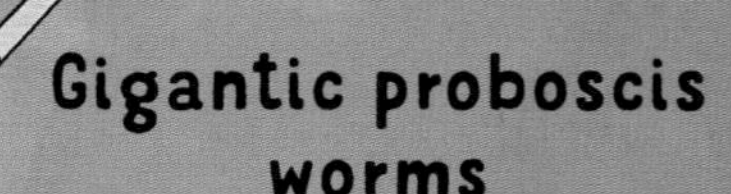

Giant sea spider

The cold, deep Antarctic water is rich in oxygen. This allows some creatures, such as sea spiders, to grow bigger here than their cousins in warmer waters.

Gigantic proboscis worms

These monster worms can grow up to 2m (6.5ft) long.

Anenome

Sea slug

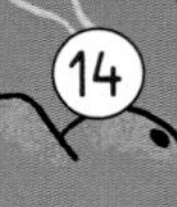

Adelie penguin
These penguins have been known to dive as deep as 180m (590ft).
The radio lets the divers talk to each other and me on the surface.
All clear up here!
Radio wire
One diver keeps watch, to make sure the other diver is safe.
The other diver makes scientific observations and collects samples.
Temperatures on Earth are rising – this is known as GLOBAL WARMING – and so the seas around Antarctica are getting warmer, too.
For this study, the divers are collecting sea stars to find out how warming water is affecting them.
Sea stars
Sea stars look cute, but they are actually hungry scavengers – gobbling up whatever they find on the seafloor.

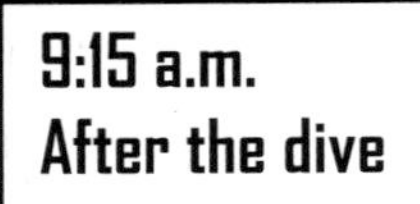
9:15 a.m.
After the dive

HONK
HONK
HONK HONK!
HONK
Ah... The majestic SERENITY of Antarctica!
These noisy Adelies spend the winter out on the sea ice, so it REALLY is much quieter then.

I love how they just wander around as if they own the place.
HONK!
HONK!
HONK!
HONK!
HONK!
Yes, it's funny until they take over the runway and our planes can't take off!

Hi little fellow! Don't get too curious, The rules* say I've got to keep away from you.
2m (6ft)

HONK!

* There are internationally agreed rules to protect the environment.

Penguins may not look graceful on land...
...and they can't fly...
HOP!
HOP!
HONK!

Body is streamlined and torpedo-shaped.
...but they really do ZIP through the water!
Flippers act like propellers underwater.
Oily feathers create a watertight layer, so water flows smoothly around their bodies.
Before I came here, I never knew there'd be so much LIFE in Antarctica.

Wildlife in Antarctica

Emperor penguins

These penguins huddle in large groups to survive the cold, dark winters.

Each penguin tucks their egg on top of their feet so it doesn't freeze on the ice.

Southern elephant seals

Male southern elephant seals battle ferociously for control over groups of females. They fight using their great weight and sharp teeth.

Skuas

Skuas nest near Rothera Station. These birds will dive at anyone who goes near their eggs, so wear a hard hat if you want to study them up close.

Blue whales

These are the largest animals that ever lived on this planet – even bigger than dinosaurs!

Belgica Antarctica

The largest insect in Antarctica is a wingless midge. It's one of only 67 species of insects recorded in Antarctica.

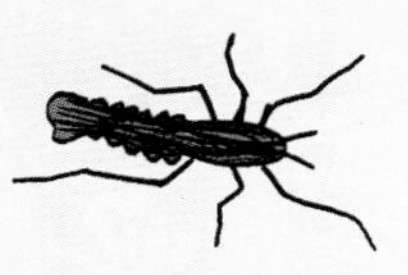

Seabird tick

These insects feed on bird blood, but only need to eat once a year.

(Before and after meal)

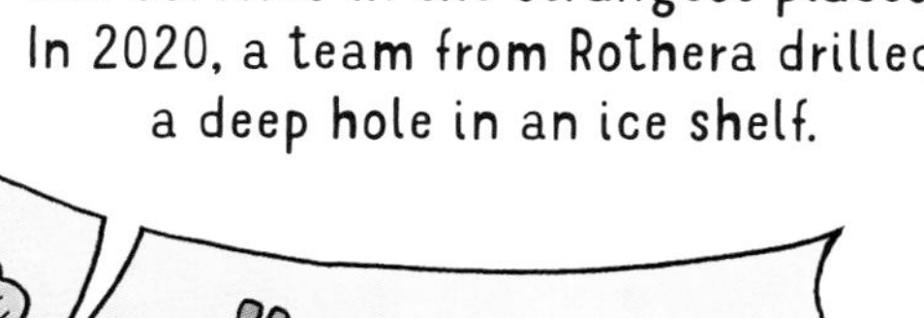

Life survives in the strangest places. In 2020, a team from Rothera drilled a deep hole in an ice shelf.
They lowered a camera to the bottom. They didn't expect to find anything alive – but they did!

Mystery creatures?

At the deep, dark bottom of the hole, miles from any source of light or food, they discovered a rock on the seabed covered in sponges and creatures that no one had ever seen before.

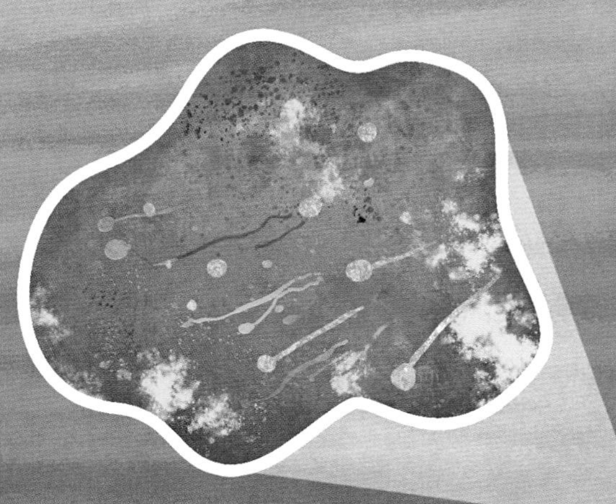

900m (3,000ft)

Hi Viv! This is Alice. Please can you come to the workshop? My drill's broken!

9:30 a.m.
Workshop
I think I've got just the right screw here.

So why do you need such a powerful drill?
I'm a geologist, so I use it to collect rock samples.

I love rocks. They can TALK if you know how to listen. And they can TRAVEL through time!

Rocks can time travel?

Yes! I use an even bigger drill to bore deep holes in the ice sheets, and take samples of the bedrock underneath.
That's the time travel part. We are digging up samples from millions of years ago.
Back then, Antarctica wasn't smothered in ice.
In fact, fossils in the rocks show us that a hundred million years ago, lots of Antarctica was covered in RAINFOREST!
So when do your rocks talk?
When we analyze these rocks in the lab, the results tell us more about what conditions were like in Antarctica when they formed.
This improves our predictions for what will happen in the future when the climate gets warmer.

SMOKO time! I made you a cuppa.
Smoko's slang round here for a tea break, right?
You got it. So Viv, what brought you to Antarctica?
Well, I always loved fixing things.
DONK
TWIST
But I didn't want to work in my parents' workshop all my life.
WHIRRRRRRRRRRRRRRRRRRRRR
So I joined the army for five years. I learned a lot there.
CRRRK CRRRK
But when I left, I wasn't sure what I wanted to DO...
Then I saw an advert for this job. It asked if I wanted to do an ORDINARY job in an EXTRAORDINARY place.

It sounded fun.
SHRUG
And it is!
Lets drink to that! So glad you're here, Viv.
CHIN-K
You've been here a while now, Alice. What do you do to chill out? Apart from talk to rocks that is?
Hah!
Don't listen to her, Blanche, she's just jealous.
SLLURRRP
Quiz nights, movie nights, skiing and snowboarding, yoga, jogging on the runway...
We have some pretty INTENSE board game sessions!
My biggest treat is to walk around "the Point". There's a bench at the top of a big cliff.
The silence there is BREATHTAKING...

...and the view isn't bad, either.
Monument to people who've died in Antarctica
Once I watched a pod of Orcas trying to knock crabeater seals off the ice for an hour.
The seals survived somehow. I couldn't believe it!
When an Orca sticks its head above water like this, it's known as SPYHOPPING.

Will you take me to the Point tomorrow after work?
Yes! I'd love to.

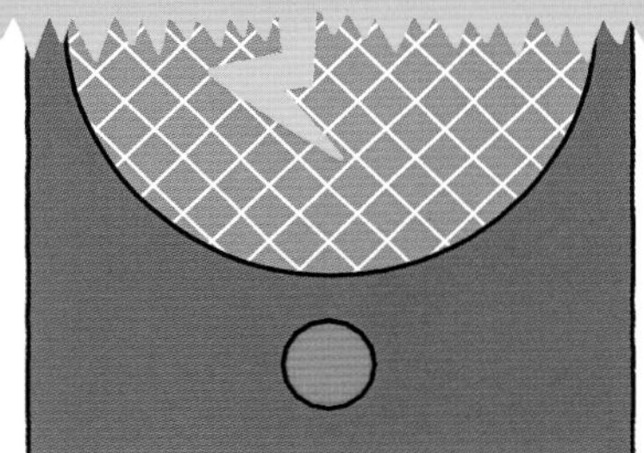
This is the station leader. A reminder that the big FOOTBALL match will start in twenty minutes.

Are you going to play?
No – it's my day in the kitchen. I've got a mound of potatoes to peel.
Everyone on the station helps cook and clean up.
Good luck! Hope you beat the Spaniards!

Oo...um. Not sure I'm ready for this.

Oop! Don't mind me sir!
Sewage treatment plant
Elephant seals can choose some funny spots for naps.

11:00 a.m.
The BIG match
Let's GO, ROTHERA!
VAMOS, ESPAÑA!
The ground isn't slippery, as it's too warm for ice.
The ground IS hard and rocky. (Viv might regret not covering up her knees...)

SHOOT, VIV!

GOOOAAALLL

Players of many talents...

Jon Hodges

Striker (Field guide)
Jon has climbed Everest.

Luz Rojas

Godlie (Ecologist)
Luz is doing a study on plastic pollution in Antarctica.

Ajay Singh

Left wing (Space physicist)
Ajay studies Earth's magnetic field.

Bruce Saxon

Right back (Pilot)
Bruce has worked in Antarctica twelve times.

12:45 p.m.
The Spanish team sails away...
See you in three months. We'll win the next one!
Adios!
It's great how friendly everyone is down here!
HESPERIDES
133
Antarctica's so remote, we HAVE to rely on each other.
When there's an emergency, every country's station does ALL they can to help.
Chinese helicopter evacuating ill Australian from Davis Base in 2020
That's cool!
It's made a lot easier by the Antarctic Treaty. I'll explain as we walk to lunch. You must be starving after running so much!

A peaceful continent

In December 1959, representatives from twelve countries signed an agreement known as the Antarctic Treaty.

The Treaty created a natural reserve, devoted to peace and science.

This mirror ball is known as the Ceremonial South Pole.
It is actually a few paces away from the real Pole.

It is one of the most successful international agreements ever made. The countries promised that Antarctica would never be a scene of conflict.

Today, 54 countries are signed up to the Treaty. It keeps Antarctica unique: a whole continent, peaceful and undisturbed.

1:00 p.m.
Lunchtime
Living in Antarctica seems to involve lots of changes of clothes. Today, I think I've swapped shoes seven times already.

Antarctica makes you HUNGRY too. I need five meals a day here, at least!

Everyone always eats together.
YUM
How much time have you spent in Rothera?
This is my... eighth? No, ninth summer! But not all in a row.

Heard you scored, Viv! How's the grub?
CHOMP
My COMPLIMENTS to the chef! And the potato peeler!
Very tasty!

STATION LEADER, STATION LEADER, Ops here. OVER
ROGER. This is station leader. What's the situation? OVER
The radar team have had a skidoo BREAK DOWN. They're out on the ice shelf. The weather doesn't look good. OVER
COLIN. Get an OTTER plane prepped. You fly in an hour.
SUE. I'll need a weather report fast. How long till the storm hits? Let me know in the comms tower.
GULP
BOB. I want you to be the FIELD GUIDE on this mission.
And VIV! Pack your tools. I'm sending you out too. Don't worry, you're READY for this!
ULP

You OK, Viv? All set for your first emergency call-out.
I'm OK Bob, I'm... ready. I'm EXCITED!
Great! As your field guide, MY job is to keep you safe enough to do YOUR job, alright?
First thing. Make sure you have your personal gear. TRIPLE check that. Don't forget spare socks!
Spare socks. Got it!
I'll get our pre-packed bags out of the store and load the plane. I'll see you in the hangar in half an hour.
And don't forget CHOCOLATE either!
Crumbs. Am I really ready? What about that storm? I'd better get packing!

HMPHHH
VIV

RRRRMMM
RRRRMMM

Viv's expedition gear

Personal stuff

Fleece middle layers of various thicknesses
Woollen hats (Viv knitted these.)
Windproof salopettes
Protective sunglasses
Gloves
Wool base layer (shirts and longjohns)
Windproof jackets
Spare underpants
Toothbrush
Whistle
Compass
Sturdy, hard-toed boots
Radio
Extra toilet paper
Toolbag
Water bottle

Camping equipment

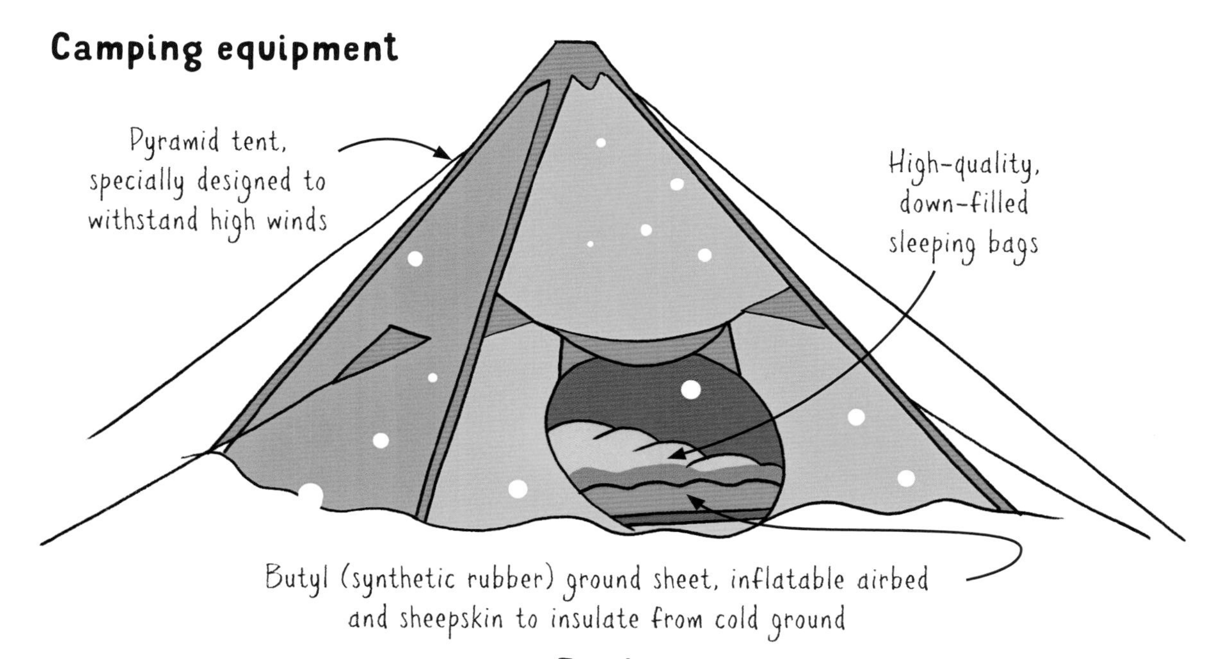
Pyramid tent, specially designed to withstand high winds
High-quality, down-filled sleeping bags
Butyl (synthetic rubber) ground sheet, inflatable airbed and sheepskin to insulate from cold ground

Food

Standard ration boxes feed one person for twenty days. They provide a balanced and varied diet of around 3,500 kilocalories for each person daily. Here's some of the things in the box.

Vacuum-packed porridge
Butter
Freeze-dried or dried main meals
Sardines
Cookies
Dried vegetables
Chocolate
Several varieties of dried soup
Rice
Dried milk
Paraffin-fired stove for cooking
Sugar
Teabags
Coffee
Drinking chocolate

2:00 p.m.
The flight should take about three hours.

My advice is grab some sleep while you can.

2:05 p.m.

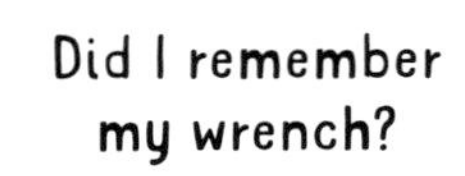
Did I remember my wrench?

Will we make it in time?
What if we get caught in a blizzard?

ZZZZ
Maybe this will distract me?
ALL ABOUT TWIN OTTERS

TWIN OTTER
Range: 1,435km (892miles)
Maximum speed: 240km (150 miles) per hour
Capacity: Pilot plus max four mission operators/scientists
Skis for landing on snow. They can be lifted to land on gravel in Rothera.
There are four Twin Otters at Rothera.
Engines: Twin turbo prop
Wing span: 19.8m (65ft)
Length: 15.7m (52ft)
Twin Otters are rugged and reliable. They need very short runways, which makes them ideal for Antarctica.
At least the view's INCREDIBLE.
HONK!

So we will be fine. Still, be ready for surprises. Always pays to respect the weather.

And put on sunscreen!

Once, I was TRAPPED in my tent for 11 days straight.
Wind howling, snow piling up. Couldn't see my NOSE in front of my FACE.
Even had to use the COMPASS to find the toilet tent.
Bob

You're not really HELPING, Bob.
Or there was the time we flew into a site we'd camped the season before.
But there was nothing to be seen! The camp had VANISHED.

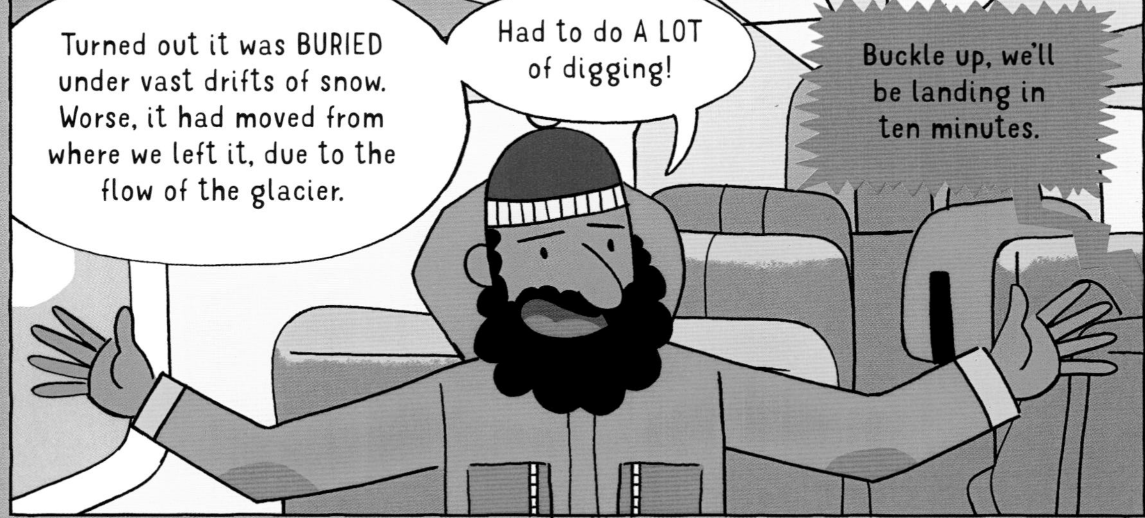
Turned out it was BURIED under vast drifts of snow. Worse, it had moved from where we left it, due to the flow of the glacier.
Had to do A LOT of digging!
Buckle up, we'll be landing in ten minutes.

4:55 p.m.
On the Larsen Ice Shelf
Oo-er! The wind's picking up.
Black flags mark out the skiway, or runway.
Twin Otters can land on very short, snowy runways – as long as they are flat and free of crevasses.
These lines are "sastrugi" – wavelike patterns made in the snow by the wind.

Hi, Viv. I'm Maria, the field guide. It's my skidoo that's broken down. We're stuck without it.

And I'm Sam, the glaciologist. Thanks for coming to save our bacon!
Hi, Sam. How long before the storm hits?
HMPH!
Time is tight! Viv and Bob need to get their tent up before the storm. Colin can't fly away until they do.
You can see it coming. Less than an HOUR, I'd say.
High Cirrus clouds trail before a storm.
SSSSSSSS
SSSSSSSS
SSSSSSSS
SSSSSSSS
SSSSSSSS
The wind begins to hiss across the ice as the storm approaches.
Better dig a pit so we can get our tent up sharpish.
For sure, I remember this from my training.
Good plan. I can help.

How to put up a pyramid tent in eight easy steps

1. Assess prevailing wind direction by looking at sastrugi.

2. Dig a square, level pit in the snow.
Ice blocks will be used later.

3. Dig diamond-shaped holes in the corners for the poles.

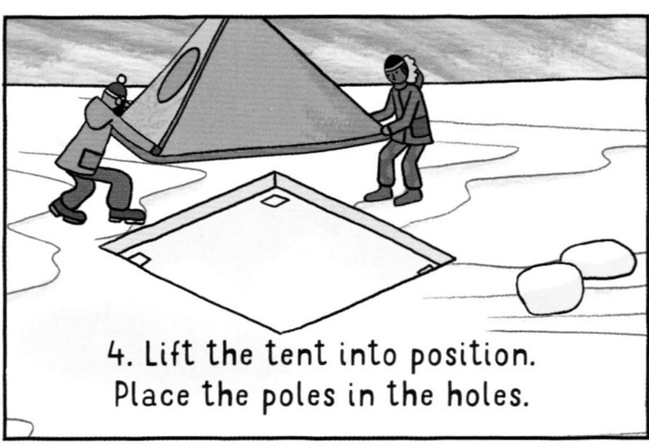
4. Lift the tent into position. Place the poles in the holes.

5. Stretch out the guy ropes and peg them in.

6. Pack the pole holes with snow.

7. Place equipment and ice blocks on the ground sheet to weigh it down.

PING
8. Tighten the ropes to fine-tune the tension.

You stack the last blocks of ice around the edge. I'll make it comfy inside.
The tents are orange so they can be seen clearly.
Inside the tent
1 Cook box
2 Paraffin-fired stove
3 Metal spill tray
4 Food boxes
5 Radio
6 Personal gear
7 Container for water
8 Snow brush
9 Emergency equipment
10 Ice blocks
Fastest pitch I've ever done. Can't believe it's your first time.
I can't believe you've already made tea!
1
2
3
4
5
6
7
8
9
10

Knock! Knock! I'm still no good at crawling through these doors.
Pyramid tents are double-walled. This helps to prevent condensation, but makes them hard to enter elegantly.
Lovely tea! Maria will be along soon. She's building us a toilet.
Awesome! How are you doing? What happened out there?
A lot better now I know we're safe...
...but it was a CLOSE-RUN thing...

We were going out to measure the depth of the ice shelf.
I was in the back, dragging the sled behind my skidoo.
We have to drive carefully. Maria was up ahead, watching out for CREVASSES.
Skidoos are linked by ropes for safety.
Well, she found one.
Suddenly she was on the edge of a SHEER DROP. I thought she was a goner.
But she SMASHED her skidoo into reverse, just in time.
CRRRK
CRRRRRRK
CRRRRKKK
TWANG
But that JOLT must have done something to her engine, because a while later, we broke down.
Hello! Any tea left?

Glaciology (ice science) with Sam

While we're having tea, let me tell you all about ice, and the research station where I worked last season.
Halley 6
This is a state-of-the-art, British research lab constructed on a floating ice shelf in the Weddell Sea. Ice shelves form over the sea.
When the ice becomes unstable, the whole station can be taken apart and moved to a safe spot.
Science pods
Power generator pods
Living pod
Sleeping pods
Up to 60 scientists can work at Halley 6 – though only 20 are there through the winter. They study the ice shelf, the weather on Earth and in space, and the ozone layer.
Ice cores
Ice sheets in Antarctica have formed in layers over many centuries. Ice sheets form over land.
Layers in the ice give us clues about the climate in the past.
Scientists drill into the ice to extract long poles known as ice cores.
The deeper they drill, the older the ice.
The oldest ice ever drilled in Antarctica was 800,000 years old.
Scientists compare the water, the chemicals, and the air bubbles of the different layers in each core. From this they can work out what the climate was like when the ice was first frozen.

Icefin
I'm so excited about ICEFIN. It's a small robot made by an American university.
Icefin can visit places no one has been to before – exploring the ocean beneath ice shelves and learning about new life.
1m (3ft)
Icefin can enter the ice vertically through very small holes. Then it uses advanced sensors to obtain as much information about conditions below the ice as possible.
Its future is even more extreme. The technology is being tested so that Icefin can explore other oceans in our solar system, such as the ones on Jupiter's moon Europa.
I hope it finds evidence of life!
Sam, you might have to stop talking now.
We have to scamper back to our tent before the storm hits.
Sorry! We haven't seen anyone in a month. I'm probably GOING ON.
Don't worry! It's fascinating. Good luck out there!

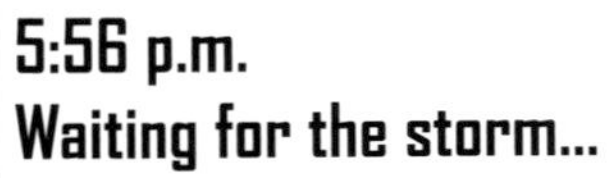

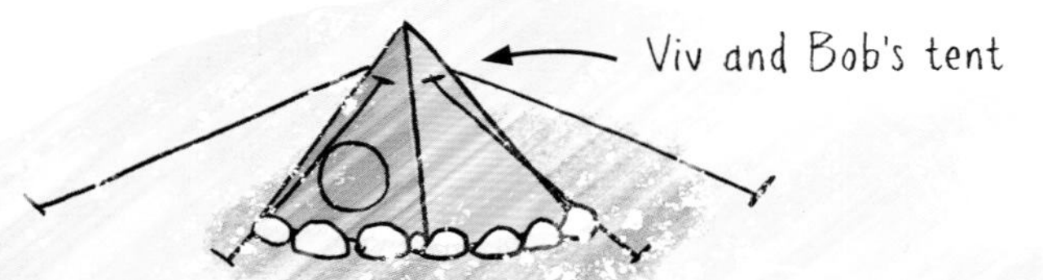

Viv and Bob's tent

The tents can withstand winds up to 100km (62m) per hour in full blizzard conditions.

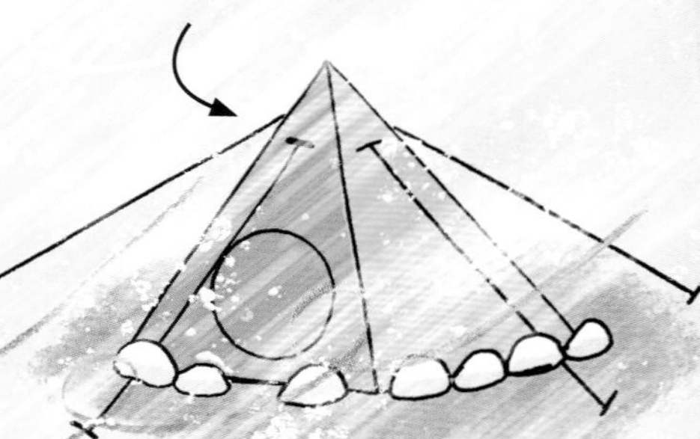

Bob talks about Antarctic weather

Antarctica is the coldest, windiest and driest continent on Earth.

The LOWEST temperature ever recorded on the Earth's surface was -89.2°C (-128.6°F) at Vostok station on 21st July, 1983.

In the extreme cold, each breath is painful. You have to take care not to freeze part of your throat or lungs when breathing in.

Over the ice shelves, MASSIVE concentrations of cold air build up.

Gravity pulls that cold air downhill. This is known as a KATABATIC WIND. These winds can be hurricane force.

Katabatic storms can last for weeks on end.

There's not much snowfall here at all, making Antarctica the world's LARGEST desert.
Often, what looks like a snow storm is just old fallen snow blowing about.

Antarctica is the world's HIGHEST continent above sea level. HUGE mountain ranges are buried under ice sheets that can be up to 4,500m (15,000ft) thick.

The higher you go, the colder it gets. BRRR!

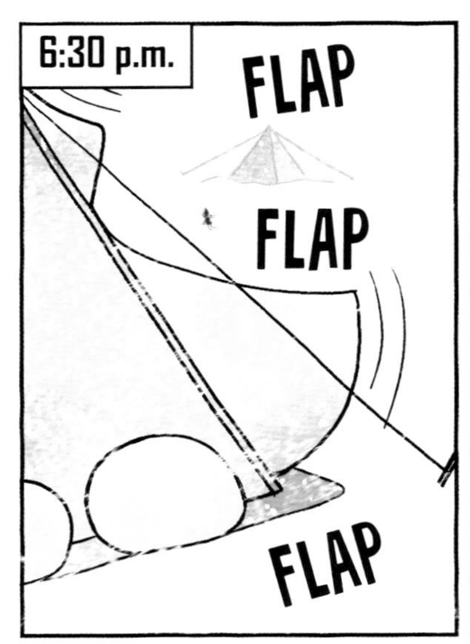
6:30 p.m.
FLAP
FLAP
FLAP

The stove is always on to melt ice for drinking, cleaning and cooking. This also heats the tent.

6:45 p.m.
Somehow soup always tastes better in a tent.

6:50 p.m.
I can't believe how warm it is in here now!
FWHOOOOOOO

... or how little elbow room we have!
BUMP

Ha
Ha
Ha
Ha
Ha
Ha

7:30 p.m.

Funny what you get used to! Now where did I put my book?

GREAT ANTARCTIC JOURNEYS

Amundsen's 1911 expedition – the first to reach the South Pole

Roald Amundsen was a Norwegian explorer.

19th October: Five men and 52 dogs began the journey.

It took them a month to cross the Ross Ice Shelf.

17th November: They reached the Transantarctic Mountains. They searched for a way through. Eventually they found a route up a steep glacier. It was a tough climb – the snow was very soft.

The explorers wore clothes made from reindeer and wolf skin.

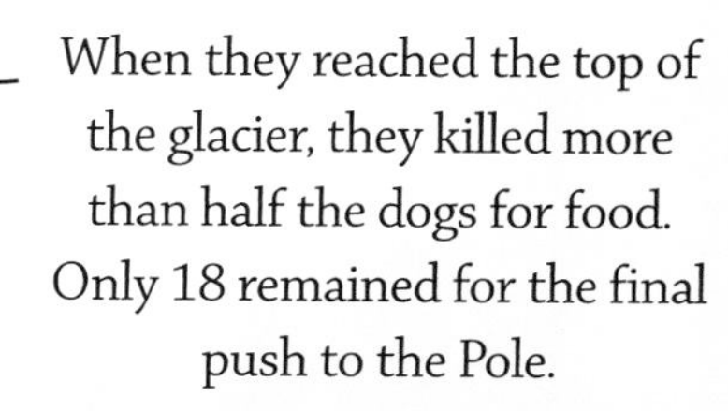

When they reached the top of the glacier, they killed more than half the dogs for food. Only 18 remained for the final push to the Pole.

25th November: This was one of the toughest sections of the route, full of snow-masked crevasses. Amundsen called it "the Devil's Ballroom".

12th of December: Amundsen thought he saw a black speck on the horizon and worried that he had been overtaken. It turned out to be dogs' droppings, magnified by a mirage.

SOUTH POLE

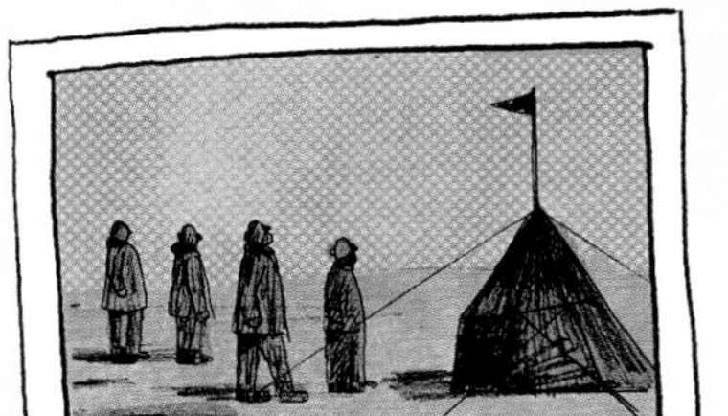

14th December: Amundsen and his team raised the Norwegian flag at the South Pole. They were the first people to reach it.

8:45 p.m.
I think it might be calming down a LITTLE.
Must be. I can HEAR you and you're not shouting!

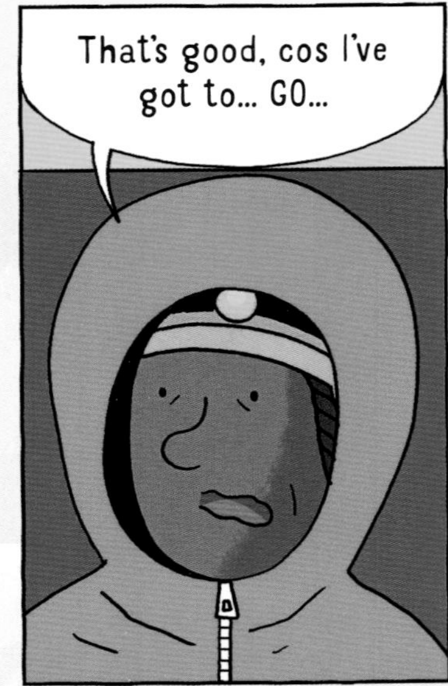
That's good, cos I've got to... GO...

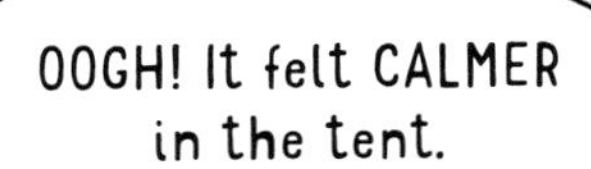
OOGH! It felt CALMER in the tent.

HOOOOOO
OOOWWWWWWWWWWLLLLL

Wooden seat so you don't stick to it in cold weather
Bucket

Ice wall shelters from wind and gives privacy

USING THE TOILET IN ANTARCTICA: THE BASIC FACTS

- Because Antarctica is so cold, any waste that we leave doesn't degrade.
- Antarctica has to be maintained as a pristine environment.
- Expeditions are careful to remove as much human waste and trash as possible.
- The waste buckets are flown back to Rothera for processing.

TOP TIPS

- If you need to go at night, it's much easier to stay in the tent and use a bottle.
- Label your drinking water bottle and your waste bottle clearly so they can't be confused.

- Stick the bottle at the bottom of your sleeping bag to keep it warm. Liquids expand when they freeze. You don't want a waste bottle to explode in your tent.
- Remember to screw the bottle top tight!

Thank goodness for the rope! I can hardly see.

How was it? Frozen bottom?
Cold! And there's definitely a STORM still!

And now I have to get my boots off AGAIN!
Laces are fiddly with gloves on.

8:55 p.m.
Rothera has a nightly radio check with every field party.
This is Rothera. How are things, Viv? OVER
Things are super, thanks! The storm is so exciting! OVER

I've good news: the storm should BLOW THROUGH tonight. You'll have a DINGLE day tomorrow: clear sky and sunshine. OVER

Fab. Just hope I can fix that skidoo. OVER
GREAT STUFF. Goodnight then you two! OVER
High frequency field radios are reliable for communicating over long distances.

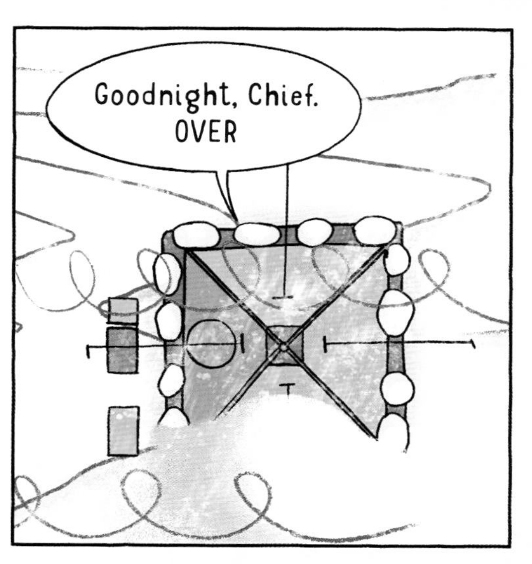
Goodnight, Chief.
OVER

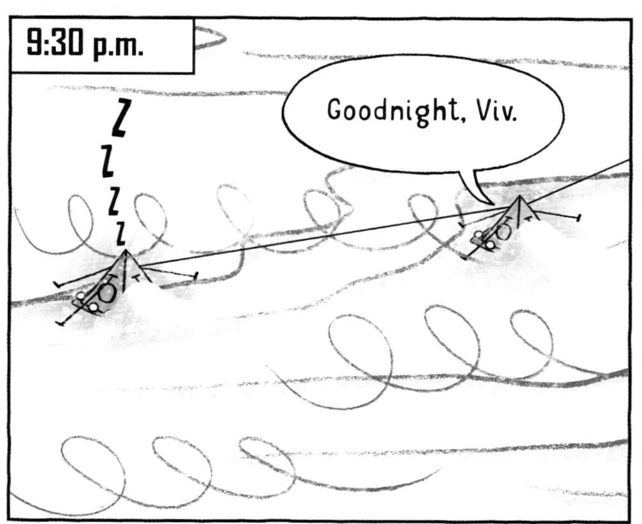
9:30 p.m.
Z Z Z Z
Goodnight, Viv.

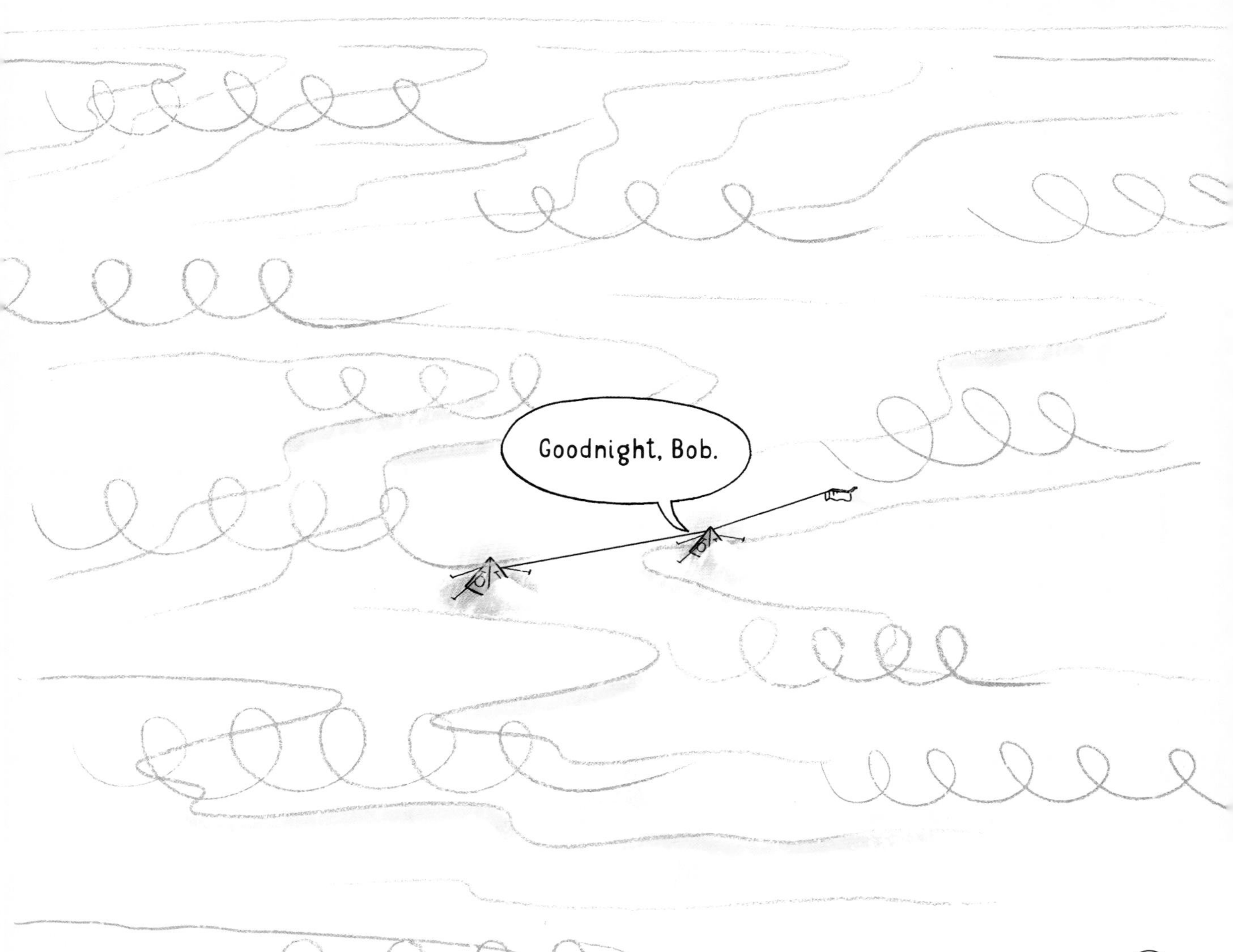
Goodnight, Bob.

5:30 a.m.
Why is it so quiet?
WAH! WHERE AM I!
Morning, Viv. I made coffee!
Something's different?
The wind has STOPPED!
Up and at 'em! Don't forget the sunscreen.

This is our radar sled. It enables us to map the bottom of the ice shelf and see if it's melting.

The radar equipment sends radio waves through the ice.

Larsen Ice Shelf

Ocean

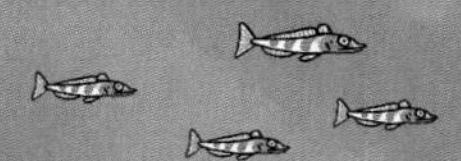

The radio waves are reflected when they hit the water, which shows the depth of the ice shelf.

Our measurements show the ice is melting. That's because temperatures in some areas have risen by 2.5°C (4.5°F) over the last 50 years.

Rising air temperatures mean the sea becomes warmer too, so the ice shelves are melting from above and below.
And they are BREAKING UP.
In 2017, a crack in the Larsen Ice Shelf created one of the LARGEST recorded icebergs. It was TWICE the size of Luxembourg.

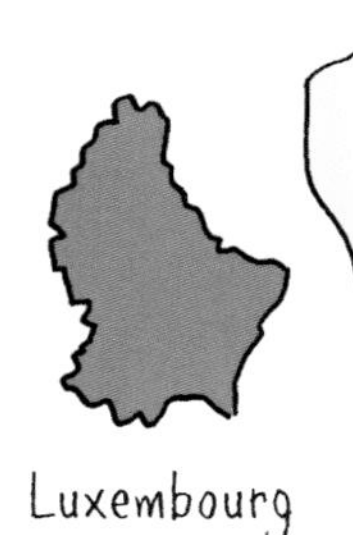
Luxembourg
Iceberg

I guess you'd call that a Luxem-berg?
HAAHAHA
But seriously...

...if the ice shelves break up, more ice from Antarctica will start to slide faster into the sea. And that will melt as well.
And what would happen then?
Well... sea levels will rise. By 2100, a lot of the world's low-lying land could be underwater.
So the more we know about it, the BETTER!
And that's why we're out here, hundreds of miles from anyone else!

So... the good news is I've fixed your skidoo!
FAB! Shall we take it for a test drive?
I'd LOVE that! Have we got time?
Our plane will be here in an hour, you're good. I'll pack things up, Viv.
Off we GO!
What an AWESOME place!
When you are out alone in this vastness. That's when you really realize how TINY you are.

Yes! It's like nowhere else. And so few people get to SEE it.

You know, if every day in Antarctica is as amazing as the last 24 hours...

...this year is going to be INCREDIBLE!

GLOSSARY

This glossary explains some of the words used in this book.

BEDROCK – Hard rock that lies underneath loose materials such as earth, or ice.

CLIMATE – How the weather in a particular place tends to be over a long period of time.

CREVASSE – A deep, open crack in ice.

DINGLE WEATHER – British Antarctic Survey slang for good weather.

FIELD GUIDE – An expert in Antarctic survival who helps scientists on expeditions beyond research stations.

GEOLOGIST – A scientist who studies rocks.

GLACIOLOGIST – A scientist who studies natural phenomena involving ice.

GLOBAL WARMING – The idea that the average temperature of the Earth has been getting hotter in recent years.

GRAVITY – The force that pulls objects to each other. The gravity of larger objects is more powerful than smaller ones.

HANGAR – A shelter for planes.

ICE SHEET – A thick layer of ice covering land.

ICE SHELF – A thick layer of ice that is floating over the ocean.

KATABATIC STORM – A strong storm caused by gravity pulling cold air downhill.

PIONEER – Someone who explores a new area.

POLAR – To do with the Earth's North or South poles.

SASTRUGI – Long, wavelike ridges of snow or ice, formed by the wind.

SEASON – The period of time that people often spend in Antarctica, usually a summer (3-6 months).

SKIDOO – A small tracked vehicle with skis used to travel on snow or ice.

SKIWAY – A runway on ice or snow that planes with skis can land on.

SMOKO – British Antarctic Survey slang for a tea break.

SOUTHERN LIGHTS - Shimmering displays of lights in the sky that sometimes appear in the Southern Hemishphere.

STATION – A collection of buildings in Antarctica where people live and work.